Interviews For Beginners

An informative self-help book for interview beginners, including: how to answer 20 commonly asked interview questions.

By

Matthew J Burgess

Copyright

Interviews For Beginners
Matthew J Burgess

Published by Matthew J Burgess

All rights reserved
Copyright © 2014 Matthew J Burgess

This book or any portion thereof may not be reproduced or used in any manner whatsoever without the express written permission of the publisher except for the use of brief quotations in a book review. Thank you for respecting the hard work of this author.

Table Of Contents

Preface

Section 1: Your Resume

Section 2: The Interview
    2.1   Preparing for an Interview
    2.2   During the Interview
    2.3   How to end the Interview
    2.4   After the Interview

Section 3: 20 Commonly asked Interview Questions

Afterword

Review and Feedback

Note regarding the use of the word 'Resume'

In the UK, a career history document is almost always referred to as a curriculum vitae or CV for short. However the term 'resume' can also be used and has exactly the same meaning.

It is an overview of the person's experience and is generally between two and four pages in length. The CV/resume will often form the basis of the interview discussion and it should be reasonably comprehensive.

It is in the USA that a real distinction is made between these terms.

US organizations may ask for either a CV or a resume but will have very different documents in mind.

A resume is a short career overview, highlighting credentials and achievements and comprising one or two pages. The objective is often just to secure an interview and is by far the most common format used. This is comparable with a UK CV.

An American CV however, is a more complete description of a person's career, including educational details, publications from their field, presentations, awards, recognitions, affiliations etc. When candidates use the CV format it is mainly for positions within academia, science or research. For all other roles the resume is used, hence why it is the most frequent type of career document.

To avoid confusion, throughout this book the word 'resume' is used.

Preface

During my twenty year career as a freelance contractor in the Information Technology business I have attended many interviews and would now class myself as an interview veteran.

Over the years I have compiled a list of the questions that I have been most commonly asked. I have prepared answers for each of these and before attending an interview I revise for it by memorizing these answers. This way, when I get asked one of the questions, the response just rolls off my tongue.

If I get asked a question that I struggle to answer, I add that question to my list and compose an answer for it so that if I get asked the same question again – this time I will be ready! So the list of questions and answers continuously gets bigger and bigger.

Using this method I have found that you gradually get better and better at answering interview questions as there is less scope to be asked something that you have not planned for.

It is a very simple technique but a very powerful one. It works!

In recent years, during the worst recession since the Second World War it has become increasingly difficult for people to get a job. Several members of my own extended family have found themselves in this situation – bright, well-educated people desperate to land a suitable role and fulfill their potential but constantly being turned down.

When I heard that my niece was struggling to get a job I sent her my list of interview questions. She wrote answers for them and was absolutely delighted when she landed her dream job in her first interview after preparing and learning her answers. She told me that several of the questions she had planned for were asked and the interviewer was very impressed with her answers.

She then passed the questions on to some other people who also went on to get jobs. These were life changing opportunities…one led to a complete change of career and the other a complete change of life as he moved to London with his girlfriend.

After this heart-warming success I decided that other people may benefit from my experience and that is why you are reading this short self-help book today.

The book will be of particular interest to interview beginners, or people who may not have had an interview for some time, such as:

- people who have been in the same job for a long time but are now looking for a new challenge and would like to brush up on their interview skills, or

- stay-at-home mothers who are looking to return to work.

The book is divided into three sections:

- **Section 1** is all about your resume. It answers the question: "Why can I not get an interview?" and provides 6 top-tips to help you to improve your resume.

- **Section 2** discusses the interview process, including: how to prepare for an interview, how to behave during the interview, how to end the interview, and what to do after the interview.

- **Section 3** lists and analyzes my 20 commonly asked interview questions, so that you will get an insight into what interview questions you are likely to be asked and how you should answer them.

The information is presented in a simple, clear and concise way and hopefully you will find it interesting, informative and (most of all) - useful!

After reading the book, the idea is that you create your own document that includes all of the questions listed in section three. You should then write answers for each of the questions so that you have your own 'Interview Questions and Answers' document. You then need to **MEMORIZE** the answers and **REHEARSE** them.

These questions are only a starting point. Every time you go to an interview and are asked a question that you didn't answer well, you should then add that question to your document and formulate an answer for it, so the next time you get asked the same question you will have a great response lined up!

By following this method your own personal 'Interview Questions and Answers' document will become more and more comprehensive and you will find that during interviews there are less and less questions being asked that you haven't already prepared an answer for. This means that your interview performance will get better and better.

Note that full answers to my interview questions are not provided as this is a self-help book designed to make you think. Instead, the questions are analyzed and hints and tips are provided to guide you in preparing your own responses. Answers to interview questions should be personal to yourself and not something regurgitated from a book.

I hope you find the information provided here useful and it helps you to find the job of your dreams.

The most important piece of advice I can give you is to never give up. Every interview you attend is a valuable learning experience and the more you have the better you will get at them!

"Never give in - never, never, never, never!"

Sir Winston Churchill, 1941

Section 1: Your Resume

Why can I not get an Interview?

I have a simple rule:

If you are sending your resume off to lots of job applications but NOT being called up for any interviews; there is something wrong with your resume.

If you ARE being called up for interviews but not getting the job, the problem is NOT with your resume but with your interview technique.

In this chapter we will discuss the first scenario – you have sent your resume off scores of times but are not being asked to attend any interviews.

The fact that lots of different people have seen your resume but decided NOT to select you for an interview is NOT a coincidence. There is something wrong with your resume.

If you are currently in this position, my advice to you is to STOP sending your resume out immediately until you have brought it up to scratch:

Albert Einstein defined 'insanity' as:

"doing the same thing over and over again and expecting different results."

It is insane to keep sending the same resume out again and again and expecting a different result. You won't get a different result until you send a different one.

Have a good read of it. Be honest - if you were an employer and you received this resume would you want to interview the candidate?

Below are some useful tips for you to consider that will help you change it from a "we will keep you on file" resume to a "we would very much like to interview you!" resume.

Resume Tip 1: Check your spelling and grammar

The very first thing to check on your resume is your spelling and grammar.

Companies can sometimes receive hundreds of resumes when a job is advertised. They have neither the time nor the inclination to read them all and bad spelling and grammar is a sure fire way to ensure that yours goes straight in the bin.

All word processors have a spellcheck feature – has your resume been spell checked?

If English language, spelling and grammar is not your strength, ask somebody else to have a look at it as discussed below.

Resume Tip 2: Get somebody to review your Resume

A few years ago my sister-in-law was desperate to become a primary school teacher but despite having all the required teaching qualifications and applying for many jobs, she couldn't even get an interview.

Eventually she asked a friend of the family who happened to be a very experienced teacher, to have a look at the resume to see if he could shed any light on the lack of interest.

The kindly teacher responded by admitting that if his school had received her resume they would have thrown it straight in the bin. This came as a shock to my sister-in-law as she didn't think there was anything wrong with it.

However, she took his advice on board and modified her resume as per his recommendations and I am delighted to say that she is now a very happy and popular primary school teacher.

The lesson to learn from this story is that YOU may think your resume is fine but your potential employer may NOT!

Don't be ashamed to ask people for help – pride will NOT get you a job. The more people who can look at the resume and give you tips the better.

Do you know anybody who is involved in recruitment who looks at resumes every day? If so ask them to look at yours.

There are also may agencies and professionals who will review your resume as part of their service.

Resume Tip 3: Look at other people's Resumes

Have you ever seen anybody else's resume?

Many people may never have seen anybody else's but their own.

It is a very useful exercise to look at other people's resumes. Do they look like yours? Which do you prefer? Who would you employ?

The more resumes you can look at the better. Learn from each one and change yours accordingly.

Resume Tip 4: Google is your friend!

There is more information than you could ever read about resumes and interviews on the internet. Have you taken the time to read any of it?

Google is your friend – it can tell you all you need to know about writing a winning resume.

There are lots of example resumes as well as resume templates that you can use.

It is a good idea to research specifically for information relating to the industry you are applying for i.e. if you want to become a teacher; google "teacher resume".

Resume Tip 5: Use LinkedIn for Resume 'inspiration'

Hopefully you are already registered on LinkedIn. If not, why not?

For those not in the know, LinkedIn is like a Facebook for work colleagues. One of the key ingredients to a successful career is good networking.

There is some truth in the saying:

"It is not what you know but who you know."

Get yourself on LinkedIn as soon as possible and add everyone that you ever meet in the world of work. It is a great way to keep in touch with people and I guarantee you that one day one of those people will help you to get a job.

Another use of LinkedIn is to get inspiration for your resume. Many people upload their entire resume to LinkedIn and it is openly visible for anybody to look at. So search for people who work in the industry you are applying for and see if there are any good lines you could use in your own resume.

Search for people you have worked with in the past. Is their description of the work you did together better than the description you have used in your resume? If so use their description as 'inspiration' for your resume.

Resume Tip 6: Tailor your Resume to the job description: include KEYWORDS

The last tip I will give you regarding your resume is to tailor it to the job description.

Do not send the same resume out to every job application!

Lots of companies use recruitment agencies when they are taking people on. They provide the agency with a job description which the agency use in their advertisement.

Quite often the agency may have very little knowledge of the industry that they are recruiting for and may not even understand a lot of the terminology.

The way many of them select the most appropriate resumes to put forward to the company is by the use of KEYWORDS. Say for example the company have told them that they want somebody that has experience of using Microsoft Excel and Microsoft Word.

Once all the resumes are in, they will do a master search of the resumes for the keywords 'Microsoft Excel' and 'Microsoft Word'. If these words are NOT in your resume, it will not even be read.

If for example your resume says "vastly experienced in the use of Microsoft Office" – your resume may not be picked out even though you have the required experience, just because it doesn't include the keywords 'Microsoft Word' and 'Microsoft Excel' in.

So you must read the job description and make sure that the keywords that the agency may search for are included in your resume.

Let me be clear here, I am not telling you to add things to your resume that you do not have experience of, I am telling you to make sure that if you DO have the required experience – make sure the CORRECT words are in the resume, clearly stated – so that a simple search tool will not miss your resume.

Don't assume that agencies read each resume – they don't!

Section 2: The Interview

2.1 Preparing for an Interview

Fantastic news! After following the steps in Section 1 you now have a great resume.

You have applied for a job along with many other people and yours has been picked out. Out of all those people, the employer thinks that *you* may be the right person for the job, so well done!

The next stage is the interview itself; but you have a lot of work to do before that.

The key to doing well in an interview is preparation, preparation, preparation:

"Fail to prepare – prepare to fail!"

No matter how many interviews you have been to in the past and how much experience you have, I guarantee that if you do not prepare well you will NOT get the job.

I have learnt this from first-hand experience when I have been a little over confident and a little lazy before the interview and then come out the other side thinking:

"I should have done more preparation for that!"

Here are the key things that you need to do before the interview:

(a) Research the company

Quite often one of the very first questions you will be asked is:

"What do you know about the company?"

If your answer is:

"Erm, er, erm…"

Let me tell you…you might as well get your coat now because you are NOT getting the job!

An employer wants to think that you aren't just after any old job but you really, really want *their* job and as such you will know a little about their company.

I am under no illusion here, many people WILL just be after any old job. You know that and I know that but your potential employer must NOT know that.

Remember, no matter how skilled or menial the job is that you are applying for, there will be lots of other people who would love to get that job.

If you know nothing about the company, what does that tell your potential employer? It tells them that you don't really want **this** job, you just want any old job, you're not passionate about joining **this** company.

On the other hand if somebody comes in and knows all about what the company does, it shows that the person is genuinely interested in joining their company. They have taken the time to do a little research. This isn't just any old job to them it is a job that they really do want.

Who would you give the job to? It is a no-brainer.

It is very easy to do a little research about a company but it is also VERY important. If you don't take the time to do it, you won't get the job – it's as simple as that!

(b) Research the position you are applying for

After quizzing you about the company itself the next question you may be asked could be:

"What do you know about the role you have applied for?"

As discussed previously it is all about convincing your potential employer that you really want this particular job. They don't want to think that you have applied for 100 other jobs and you would accept any one of them (even if you would!).

So find out exactly what the role involves. If you applied for the job through a recruitment agency, ring them up and ask them to tell you exactly what the role involves.

Read the job advertisement very carefully. What skills and experience does it specifically state are required? Think of **EXAMPLES** to **PROVE** that you have these attributes so that you can relate these to the interviewer. It is no good just saying "Yes I can do that," you have to back it up with evidence.

You will need to convince the employer that you know exactly what the role involves and that you are the correct person for the job. Remember you are fighting for this job – don't get knocked out in the first round by not knowing what the job involves!

Would you employ somebody who doesn't know anything about the job they have applied for?

(c) *Know your own Resume*

The interviewer will have a copy of your resume in front of them. You won't.

They will be asking you questions about it – so make sure you know it!

One of the first questions that many interviewers ask is along the lines of:

"Ok, tell me about yourself; give me a brief summary of where you have been working in recent years, what your job involved and what skills were required."

I can tell you from experience that when you have worked at a few places you can soon forget exactly what you were doing a few years ago. It is embarrassing when you can't remember these basic things!

It may also arouse unfounded suspicions in the interviewer…

"Why can't they remember what they have been doing? Is it because it's not true?"

It just doesn't look professional at all when you can't remember things that are included in a resume that you wrote!

So you need to know your resume inside out but in particular:

- Which companies you worked at and in which years.
- What your job involved at each company.
- What skills you were using.

The employer will be most interested in your most recent jobs but they could ask you ANYTHING about your resume.

NOTE: If you have not yet entered the world of work the same rule applies but instead of being asked about which companies you have worked for, they may ask about your university course, school, work experience or part time jobs.

(d) Create your own 'Interview Questions and Answers' document

The main purpose of this book is to provide the reader with a list of potential interview questions that they can plan answers for.

Later on in the book are the list of twenty questions that I have been most commonly asked. Note that full answers to these questions are not provided as this is a self-help book designed to make you think. Instead, the questions are analyzed and hints and tips are provided to guide you in preparing your own responses.

I have told you what may be asked, now it is over to you!

I would recommend that you copy the questions into a Microsoft Word document or other word processor and then write your own answers. You will then have your own personal 'Interview Questions and Answers' document.

Once you are happy with the answers, you need to **MEMORIZE THEM.**

This can be quite a boring task but you only get out of something what you put into it.

If you put the effort in now you may well get the job, if you don't bother you might miss out.

Just imagine how annoyed you would be with yourself if you were asked one of the questions on the list in an interview but you gave a poor answer because you hadn't bothered preparing or learning an answer.

Conversely, imagine how pleased you would be if you HAD planned an answer and it flowed effortlessly off your tongue impressing your interviewer enough to offer you the job there and then!

Commit those answers to memory! If you are taking public transport to the interview – keep going through the answers on your journey. If you are in the car, take the questions and answers with you, arrive early and go through them again in the car park.

You must go through this process before **EVERY** interview - learn them again each time.

The main reason that people get nervous before an interview is because you are stepping into the unknown – you don't know what you are going to be asked. By using this technique, over time you WILL know most of what is likely to be asked and more importantly what your responses will be. It is like already having the answers to an exam you are going to take. It will mean that you go into the interview feeling much more confident.

(e) Practice with a friend or family member

Ask a friend or family member to help you to practice for the interview by asking you each of the questions in your 'Interview Questions and Answers' document. See what they think of your answers. If they don't like them – change them.

If you forget the answer to a question – do it again.

Practice, practice, practice.

Those answers need to be ingrained in your brain. When you are asked a question in the interview there mustn't be any 'erms.' It must be 'BANG' – there's your answer!

Remember practice makes perfect.

You should have practiced so often that your pretend interviewer even knows the answers off by heart by now!

The more you prepare and practice for the interview the less stressful the main event will be.

(f) Have a 'dry run' journey to the interview location

Consider this scenario:

You have a quick look on Google Maps and it says that your interview location is only 15 minutes away.

On interview day your appointment is 9am so you set off at 8.30 thinking you have got plenty of time. However, it is rush hour and the traffic is horrendous. You don't arrive at your interview until 9.15!

Many people wouldn't even bother proceeding with the interview. If you can't make it to the interview on time what would your time keeping be like if you actually got the job? In addition, they may have lots of people to interview and you may have missed your slot.

Even if you have an understanding interviewer who assures you not to worry about being late, you have got yourself so stressed from worrying about being late that your nerves are shot and your composure has gone! You are sweating, your tie isn't straight and you can't remember any of the answers that you have been rehearsing.

To avoid this nightmare situation have a trial run. A day or so before, pretend that you are travelling to the interview at the exact time you will be there on the real day. This way you will be reasonably confident how long the journey is going to take. You will also know exactly where the interview is taking place, how far it is from the train station or where you can park etc.

It is all about giving yourself less to worry about on the day.

You want to arrive calm, well prepared and confident not a sweating, gibbering wreck!

(g) Don't tell other people that you have got an interview

I remember when I took my driving test many years ago. Everybody knew that I was taking it. My main fear on test day was not of failing the test itself but of the embarrassment of having to tell people that I had failed.

From that day on I decided that I would always try to play events down and keep my cards close to my chest.

I have always found that the worst part of NOT getting a job after an interview is TELLING people that I didn't get the job.

If you excitedly announce on Facebook that you have got an interview but then don't get the job, you then have to report on Facebook that you DIDN'T get the job! Likewise if you tell everyone that you bump into about the interview, the next time you bump into them they will ask you how you got on…awkward!

By telling lots of people, you are putting more pressure on yourself…only tell the people that really need to know.

Keep the interview as quiet as possible. If you don't get the job…it doesn't matter…nobody knew you had the interview anyway.

If you do get the job…what are you waiting for? Make a big announcement on Facebook!

2.2 *During the Interview*

Interview day is here. You have created your own 'Interview Questions and Answers' document that includes all of the questions listed in this book and you have memorized all of the answers. You have arrived nice and early. Your preparation has been spot on.

Now it is time for the interview itself!

Let's begin with the basics:

- Be smart – no trainers!

- Shake the interviewer's hand at the start and end of the interview with a FIRM handshake.

- Try to appear professional and confident but NOT overconfident.

- Take your 'Interview Questions and Answers' document and your resume with you and spend the last few minutes before the interview having one last read of them.

Here are some other points to consider during the interview itself:

(a) This interview does not mean life or death!

I know you are nervous about the interview…let me tell you EVERYBODY gets nervous before an interview no matter how experienced they are - it is perfectly normal.

A nice thought that I always tell myself is that no matter what happens at the interview today; tonight it will all be over, for better or for worse and I will be snuggled up in front of the fire with my loved ones. (Cheesy I know but I find it helps!)

Another thing to consider is that quite often the interviewer is just as nervous as the interviewee. I have known many people who find interviewing quite a daunting experience so it's quite a calming thought to bear in mind that you may not be the only nervous person in the room.

Try not to build the interview up too much in your head. Remember, you have done fantastically well to be called up for an interview ahead of many other people.

Let's look at what are the best and worst outcomes from this interview:

The best outcome is obviously that you get the job and you are going to have a really great day!

The worse outcome is that you don't get the job. If that is the case, it is NOT the end of the world. Although you didn't get the job, attending the interview was a priceless experience that you will learn from. You now have more interview experience and next time you will be even better.

So try not to think of this interview as a life or death situation, just think of it as an opportunity to gain interview experience. If you get the job – fantastic, if you don't - learn from it.

(b) Arrive five minutes early – no earlier!

The time that people arrive for interviews seems to vary massively.

Rule Number 1 regarding the interview is **DO NOT BE LATE!** As discussed earlier in the book, many people wouldn't even bother proceeding with the interview if you are late. If you can't make it to the interview on time what would your time keeping be like if you actually got the job? They may have lots of people to interview and you may have missed your slot.

If you are late you better have a VERY good excuse!

However, almost as bad as being late in my opinion, is being extremely early. I worked somewhere recently where an interviewee announced himself at reception half an hour early! Would you arrive at the doctors half an hour early and expect to be seen? You are given an appointment time for a reason – that is the time of your appointment, not half an hour before! Your interviewer is a very busy person and being told that the interviewee has arrived half an hour early will not impress him or her it will annoy them.

Personally I like to arrive at the interview location nice and early so that I am calm and relaxed. If I am sat in the car park I then pull out my 'Interview Questions and Answers' document and spend the last few minutes rehearsing my answers again. I also have one last read of my resume to make sure that I don't get any facts confused in the interview.

Then I present myself at reception five minutes before the allotted time, this gives the interviewer time to collect me and we can begin the interview exactly on time.

So arriving in the building five minutes early is perfect…spend any time available before that doing last minute revision.

(c) Don't discuss money

I find being asked how much money I would like during an interview rather uncomfortable.

You are worried about sounding greedy but you also don't want to sell yourself short.

Personally I don't think the interview is the correct forum for discussing the salary as you may feel under pressure to agree a lower rate to ensure that you get the job.

I would expect that the job advertisement gave an indication of the salary that the company are willing to pay and/or you have discussed it with the agency, so both parties should know that a mutually agreeable salary should be easily reachable.

So the way I always answer the 'money' question is by saying:

"I am very keen on the role and my salary is negotiable."

2.3 *How to end the Interview*

You can sense that the interview is drawing to a close. You can feel the relief washing over your body and the urge to jump up, leave the room and rejoice that it is over.

However, the end of the interview is one of the most crucial points and the way you handle it may mean the difference between you getting the job or NOT getting the job.

So focus and consider the following points:

(a) Have you said everything you wanted to say?

Before the interview you created your own 'Interview Questions and Answers' document and memorized your prepared answers. Was there an answer that you felt was really important to convey during the interview but the relevant question has not been asked? i.e. maybe something you have done or experienced that may just give you the edge over your interview rivals? If so use the end of the interview to mention this.

During an interview you don't have to just sit there and answer questions and then leave. You also have an element of control.

Generally, towards the end of the interview you will be asked:

"Is there anything else you would like to ask or discuss?"

This would be the perfect time for you to say:

"One thing I would like to mention is…"

Don't come out of the interview thinking "I wish I had said this," or "If only I had told them about that."

Remember, you are trying to sell yourself during the interview so make sure you tell them all the important things about yourself that you think they should know.

Some people find it hard to say nice things about themselves but you must. An interview is all about selling yourself.

When you leave that interview room make sure you have told them all of the important things you wanted them to know. That is what the other interviewees will be doing, so if you don't do it you are putting yourself at a disadvantage.

(b) Do you have any questions about the company or the job?

Most interviews end with this question and if you say: "Erm, no I don't think so," it leaves the interviewer with the impression that you are not really that keen on this particular job or this company. Somebody who is really passionate about the role would definitely have some questions.

What the question actually means is:

"Do you really want *this* job or are you just after any old job?"

You don't need a lot of questions…ideally two but AT LEAST ONE just to show that you are definitely keen on the job. It shows that you have been thinking about it.

Some example questions are shown below:

- How many people are on the team that I will be joining if successful?

- What training will be provided?

- If you are looking to stay with the company for a long time you could ask them what the long term prospects are (i.e. promotion prospects).

Or you could ask them something specifically to do with the role or the company itself. Anything that makes the interviewer think that you are definitely keen on this particular role.

NOTE: **DO NOT ASK ANYTHING ABOUT PAY!** That is not what this section of the interview is for!

If you still require some inspiration for questions you could ask at the end of the interview there are lots of suggestions available on the internet.

(c) Ask them if there is anything THEY have concerns about

Towards the end of the interview it is possible that the interviewer is in two minds about you. They may be thinking that you MIGHT be the right person for the job but they have a slight concern.

They probably won't tell you this concern unless YOU ask THEM. So sometimes, although it is a little bit awkward, try asking this question:

"Are there any questions that you don't think I answered fully or you have concerns about?"

They might then tell you something that they are a little bit unsure about and once this is out in the open, you then have a window of opportunity to provide them with more information to ease their concern and convince them that you are DEFINITELY the right person for the job!

(d) Tell them loud and clear that you want the job

They say that you never get a second chance to make a good first impression. However, although first impressions are important, LAST impressions are equally if not MORE important.

Once the interview is over you want to leave the interviewer with the impression that you are really keen on the job and that you believe you are the right person for the role.

SO TELL THEM LOUD AND CLEAR!

Before leaving, tell them that the role sounds really interesting and that you would definitely like to work there.

The last thing you say at the end of the interview must be that you are really keen on the role.

When the interviewer completes his or his report regarding your interview you want them to say:

"This candidate seemed really enthusiastic about the role and the company."

If you leave them with that impression it will stand you in good stead.

An enthusiastic candidate will always be given the job over an equally qualified unenthusiastic candidate!

2.4 After the Interview

It's over! How did it go?

If it went well – congratulations! You deserve it because of all the preparation that you put in BEFORE the interview.

If it didn't go so well, don't get too down about it. As we agreed earlier you should look upon each interview as an experience to learn from. Quite often you learn more from a bad experience than you do from a good one.

(a) Why did I not get the job?

Sometimes your interview can go as well as it possibly could have done but unfortunately there was another candidate, who on this occasion was slightly more suited to the role than yourself. You may have been second choice out of all the candidates and would have been offered the role if that other person hadn't also applied. So an element of luck and chance is sometimes involved.

Another point to bear in mind is that interviews can be quite subjective and the outcome can vary greatly depending on the personalities in the interview room.

I will give you an example of this. I was once being interviewed by two people and all the way through the interview, as I answered their questions, one of the interviewers was nodding his head in agreement and smiling; at the same time the other interviewer was shaking his head and frowning. It was a strange experience!

After the interview, the agency called me to ask how it had gone and they asked me if they thought I would be offered the job. I told them that it depended on which one of the interviewers had the final say! (As it happens I did get offered the job!).

My point is that whether you get the job or not can sometimes depend on the personality of the person interviewing you. In my example above, if I was only being interviewed by the person shaking his head I would NOT have been offered the job whereas the other interviewer WOULD have offered me the job.

So if you didn't get the job, don't beat yourself up. Now is NOT the time to feel down, now is the time to learn from the interview experience and make sure that you improve next time…

(b) Add any new questions to your 'Interview Questions and Answers' document

This is the key to the whole book!

As soon as you have returned home from your interview, write down any questions that you were asked, that you don't feel you answered particularly well.

Add the questions to your own personal 'Interview Questions and Answers' document and then plan a GOOD answer for it.

The next time you are asked the same question in an interview you will have a well-rehearsed response ready and the interviewer will say "Excellent answer!"

Do you see now why each interview is a valuable experience? The more interviews you attend, the more questions and answers will go in your document and the better prepared you will be next time.

Each interview is a dress rehearsal for the next one!

It is a process of continuous improvement.

If you keep updating your document and keep learning the answers before the next interview you will reach a point where there is almost nothing that can be asked of you for which you don't have a prepared answer.

Section 3: 20 Commonly asked Interview Questions

This section lists the 20 generic questions that I have been asked most often during interviews.

I have not included questions that are related to the particular industry that I work in (IT) as they will not be relevant to most people.

You should copy these questions into your own 'Interview Questions and Answers' document, prepare answers for them and learn them.

Note, however, that these questions are just a starting point. Every time you go to an interview and are asked a question that is NOT in the list you should ADD that question to your document and write a good answer for it ready for next time.

For example, you will need to add questions that are specific to the particular industry that you work in. By doing this you will end up with a comprehensive, personalized document containing good answers for all the questions that you are likely to be asked in future interviews.

Remember, the whole theme of this book is about continuous improvement i.e. learning from experience and getting better and better with each interview that you attend.

As mentioned earlier in the book, full answers to the questions are NOT provided. Instead, the questions are analyzed and hints and tips are provided to guide you in preparing your own responses. The questions are here to provoke thought and help YOU to devise good, unique and personal answers that will impress your interviewer.

The Questions

1. What do you know about the company and why do you want to work for us?

If you know nothing about the company it tells your potential employer that you don't really want *this* job and you're not passionate about joining *this* company - you just want any old job.

On the other hand if you know all about what the company does it shows that you are genuinely interested in joining their company as you have taken the time to do a little research. This isn't just any old job to you - it is a job that you really do want.

2. What do you know about the role?

As per question one this is about proving that you are really interested in this particular job.

3. Give EXAMPLES to prove you have the required skills for this job.

Quite often in interviews, rather than just asking "Have you got this skill," or "have you done this," they ask you to give them **EXAMPLES** to **PROVE** that you have got the skills or experience they require.

So before the interview you need to study the job specification to see what skills or experience they are looking for. Then think of examples you can tell them about, to PROVE that you have these attributes.

For example, instead of saying "Yes I have used Microsoft Excel," you could say "I used Microsoft Excel in my previous job to keep basic accounts. In doing so I learnt how to use Excel to calculate totals."

4. Give me a brief summary of where you have been working in recent years, what your job involved and what skills were required.

You need to know your resume inside out but in particular:

- Which companies you worked at and in which years.
- What your job involved at each company.
- What skills you were using.

If you have not yet entered the world of work the same rule applies but instead of being asked about which companies you have worked for, they may ask about your university course, school, work experience or part time jobs.

5. Describe a situation where you have had conflict at work or where you have resolved conflict between two people.

Conflict is a common occurrence in the workplace. There are lots of different personalities and egos and sometimes they clash.

The interviewer wants to know how you would handle dealing with difficult people at work. They don't want to employ somebody who might have big arguments or fights in the workplace.

To say that you have NEVER had any conflict in your life because you are such a good people person is not a good answer because:

(a) it is not really believable and
(b) it doesn't tell them how you would respond if you DID meet a difficult person in the workplace.

They may even have a person in the team that you are applying to join, who they **KNOW** is very difficult to work with and they want to find out how you would deal with them.

The kind of person they are looking for is probably somebody who resolves conflict by perhaps taking the other person into a quiet room, having a private chat and sorting the problem out **personally** and **professionally**.

So think of an example where you have handled and resolved a clash in a similarly calm way. It doesn't matter if this was in work, education or in your personal life.

6. Give an example of when you have had a challenging situation at work.

There are many ways that you could answer this question.

If you haven't already used it, you could give the answer that you have prepared for question five above, regarding a time where you encountered conflict in the office.

Or, you could talk about a period of time when your workload was very high and how you handled it.

It is not the challenging situation itself that is important – it is what **YOU** did to **OVERCOME** the situation that the interviewer is really interested in. So make sure that you paint yourself in a good light.

7. What is your weak point?

This is the question that people struggle the most with - if they haven't prepared an answer for it. To answer this well, on the spot, without any time to think about it is very difficult.

You have spent the whole interview selling yourself and telling your prospective employer how good you are and then all of a sudden you are asked to say something bad about yourself.

"Erm, um, I can't really think of anything," is a poor, awkward, embarrassing answer.

However, you DO have to be really careful when answering this question. You could easily trip yourself up and the wrong answer could lead to a rejection.

For example, if you are applying to be a bomb disposal engineer the following answer would immediately lead to a finger pointing at the exit door:

"My weak point is that I am color blind!"

The key to answering the question is to **turn the negative into a positive** as shown in the example below:

"One thing that I have never really enjoyed is public speaking - I used to get quite nervous beforehand. So in order to improve I have put myself forward to do some presentations recently and have gained much more confidence and received good feedback. In fact earlier this year I was best man at a wedding and had to do a speech in front of 100 people and it went down really well."

This response is very clever because instead of telling them what your weak point IS, you are telling them what your weak point

USED TO BE and what you have done to overcome it and turn it into a strength.

One final point regarding this question is: please don't say "I am a perfectionist." This is a common answer but is such a cliché and whilst you may think it paints you in a good light, in reality it may not.

Being a perfectionist implies that you probably spend a long time doing each task - probably too long. In the job that you are applying for there may be so much work to do that you simply won't have time to do everything perfectly because you will be too slow and hold the team up.

8. What do you feel are your best achievements inside or outside of work?

The answer to this will be personal to you but where possible try to mention something that has relevance to the role that you are applying for.

For example if you are applying for a team leader role, a relevant achievement would be that you once took over as manager of a poor performing team and turned them into the best performing team.

Achievements outside of work can also show that you have the skills required for the job; if you are the manager of a successful football team for instance.

9. Why should we employ you?

Remember, you have to sell yourself in an interview – don't be modest! You are competing against other candidates and have to convince the interviewer that you are more suitable to the job than them.

There are many answers you could give for this and some examples are listed below:

- You have the relevant skills and experience.
- You have held a very similar role before and have excelled in it.
- You are keen to learn and hard working.
- You can hit the ground running.

10. What kind of people do you like working with?

This is another tricky question.

The interviewer is considering whether they think you would fit into their work environment or not and if you give the wrong answer it could lead to your name being crossed out.

Let's say that unbeknownst to you, most of the people in the workplace that you are applying for are mature people who have been there for many years and you reply:

"I like to work with young, dynamic people."

This may lead the interviewer to think that you wouldn't be happy in this particular job.

So try not to be too specific - sometimes it is better and perfectly acceptable to give quite vague answers. You basically want to give the impression that you like working with ALL types of people. More importantly, you don't want to confess that there is a certain type of person that you DON'T like working with because if there is a person like that in the team you applying for, you may have just talked yourself out of a job!

So a generic response similar to this would be suitable:

"I have worked with many different types of people in my career (education) so far. Obviously, it is always nice to work with friendly, like-minded people but everyone is different and that is one of the things that makes the workplace so interesting. I have excellent people skills and understand that you have to treat people in different ways in order to forge a good working relationship with them"

11. How do you like to be managed?

Just as in the last question, make sure that you don't put your foot in it with the wrong answer.

You probably don't know how you would be managed if you got the job so you have to be very careful that you don't rule yourself out with the wrong response. You need to cover all bases with your answer to give the impression that you can work under any type of management.

An example answer could be:

"In my current role my manager simply tells me the work that needs to be done and when the deadline is. I am then trusted to get the work done on time and have been very effective in doing so.

However, I am very adaptable and have worked successfully under many different management styles. Different managers work in different ways and it is simply a case of adjusting your way of working in order to fit in and produce the best results."

With this answer you have hinted at the way you like to be managed but you have added a caveat to say that you can work under **ANY** management type.

12. Are you passionate about your job?

The answer is '**YES!**"

In reality, many people are NOT passionate about their jobs but you cannot admit or portray that.

You have to respond that you ARE passionate about your job and also tell them why.

Is there a part of your job that you really enjoy? For example, meeting lots of different people or learning new skills.

13. How would you handle a situation where you have too much work to do? For example, if two different managers are telling you that they need their work finished now and you simply don't have time to do BOTH.

It is not unusual for workers to find themselves, through no fault of their own, in a situation where they have too much work to do and not enough time to do it in and hence it is a legitimate question to ask how you would cope in this scenario.

Do NOT say:

"I never get behind with my work and if I did I would simply work harder to get it all done."

Whilst you are trying to sell yourself in an interview, there has to be an element of realism. No matter how good you are, it is still possible that under certain circumstances you might find yourself under strain and your prospective employer wants to know how you would react.

They need to know that you would be able to act calmly and decisively to resolve the situation, rather than keeping it all to yourself and ending up having to take time off work through stress.

I once worked for a company where we each had to deal with a large amount of postal correspondence every day. One member of the team was always completely up to date with her work and never once asked for help.

However, we started receiving lots of complaints from customers asking why they hadn't received a response to their letters. The manager found this baffling as there was no outstanding post at all.

One day when the employee in question had a day off, somebody looked in her drawers and found that they were stacked high with unanswered post!

When she was confronted about this, she broke down in tears and confessed that she had been incredibly stressed and couldn't keep up with her workload. Rather than asking for help she had started hiding the post in her drawers and it snowballed from there.

That is exactly how NOT to behave when you find yourself with too much work to do!

When the workload becomes too much, you have to swallow you pride and ask for help. Bottling up the stress only leads to one thing – time off work and poor health.

A study conducted by the International Stress Management Association found that more than half of people in work had suffered from stress over a period of a year. Also, statistics have shown that a quarter of working people have taken time off sick due to stress and that stress is the leading cause of sick leave. Each new case of stress leads to an average of 29 days off work.

So you can see why this is an important question. Employers don't want to take people on who are too proud to ask for help and will then end up having to take 29 days off with stress!

A good starting point to answering the question would be to say that if it is a one off unusual event then you would be prepared to work later for a short period of time or come in at the weekend in order to catch up.

However, if it is more serious or long term, you need to **REPORT IT** as soon as possible, explaining that you simply can't do everything that has been asked of you in the allotted time.

At the same time, offer **POTENTIAL SOLUTIONS** e.g. you either need more time, some help or you could **PRIORITIZE** the work i.e. you can do this piece of work but not that one.

It is perfectly fine and acceptable to ask for help!

You are only human and there are only so many hours in a day – don't carry the burden alone. Be transparent and report it.

In the situation where you have two different managers making demands of you, it would be a good idea to request a meeting with the three of you in attendance. You could then explain to them both that it is not possible to complete all of the tasks that they have requested of you within the timescale and try to reach agreement on a mutually acceptable plan of action.

14. What do you find least enjoyable about your job?

This is a very tricky question to answer and the wrong response could mean you don't get the job.

For example, if you are a teaching assistant and you reply:

"The thing that I find least enjoyable about my job is…the kids!"

The key to this question is to skillfully answer it so that you turn a negative into a positive.

Using the teaching assistant example you could say:

"The thing that I find least enjoyable about my job is the end of the year when I have to say goodbye to the kids. After spending a year working closely with them and watching them grow and develop it is a very sad day when we have to say goodbye."

15. Name an occasion where you have made a mistake.

"Anyone who has never made a mistake has never tried anything new."
Albert Einstein

Everybody makes mistakes at some point – it is nothing to be ashamed of. So don't try to impress the interviewer by saying that you have never made one.

The main purpose of the question is not to find out *why* you made the mistake but rather what you did to rectify it and learn from it.

The interviewer will want to know that you were brave enough to hold your hands up and admit the mistake and not try to cover it up. They will be keen to hear how you reacted calmly and swiftly to resolve the error.

It is also important to point out how you **learnt from the mistake** to make sure that it wasn't repeated.

16. How do you learn new skills when you start a new job?

If the employer decides to take you on, they will want to know that you will be able to get up to speed and become productive as soon as possible. This question gives you the opportunity to explain how you would do this.

The best way to learn new skills is by asking the experienced employees to teach you.

Personally when I start a new job, I write down everything that I learn so that I can refer back to it later. When training somebody up most people are happy to explain how something is done once or twice but any more than that is infuriating.

Writing down notes is a great way of remembering and prevents you from having to ask the same thing again and again.

It might also impress the employer to say that when you start a new job you sometimes take relevant documents home in the evening to read in your own time or do research on the internet in order to learn the job specifics quicker.

17. Tell me about an experience at work where you were NOT happy and why?

Similar to some previous questions, the key here is not what the situation was that you were unhappy with but what YOU did to fix it.

The employer wants to know that when things aren't going well you are a strong enough character to cope with it and more importantly to change it.

So if you were unhappy with the conduct of a particular person, perhaps you had a private chat with them to raise your concerns and this led to a happy outcome.

Similarly, if you were beginning to feel stressed because you had too much work to do, maybe you spoke to your manager and asked for help.

Have you ever been in a situation where you didn't feel the work was challenging enough for you? If so, what did you do about it? Rather than just leaving the company, a much better solution would be to tell your manager that you are unhappy and ask for some more stimulating work. It is in an employer's interest to ensure that their employees are happy rather than risk losing them - as there is a large cost involved in recruitment.

So this question is all about what **YOU** did to turn an unhappy situation into a happy one.

18. What are your strengths?

Before the interview you need to study the job specification to see what skills or experience they are looking for.

You then need to convince the interviewer that you have these attributes.

So the strengths that you talk about should be tailored towards the role you are applying for.

19. What salary are you looking for?

Being asked the 'money' question during an interview can be rather uncomfortable.

You are worried about sounding greedy but you also don't want to sell yourself short.

The job advertisement probably gave an indication of the salary that the company are willing to pay and/or you have discussed it with the agency. So both parties should know that a mutually agreeable salary should be quite easy to reach.

So, I would answer the question by saying:

"I am very keen on the role and my salary is negotiable."

20. Do you have any questions about the job?

Most interviews end with this question and if you say: "Erm, no I don't think so," it leaves the interviewer with the impression that you are not really that keen on this particular job or this company. Somebody who is really passionate about the role would definitely have some questions.

What the question actually means is:

"Do you really want *this* job or are you just after any old job?"

You don't need a lot of questions...ideally two but AT LEAST ONE just to show that you are definitely keen on the job. It shows that you have been thinking about it.

Some example questions are shown below:

- How many people are on the team that I will be joining if successful?

- What training will be provided?

- If you are looking to stay with the company for a long time you could ask them what the long term prospects are (i.e. promotion prospects).

Or you could ask them something specifically to do with the role or the company itself. Anything that makes the interviewer think that you are definitely keen on this particular role.

NOTE: **DO NOT ASK ANYTHING ABOUT PAY!** That is not what this section of the interview is for!

If you still require some inspiration for questions you could ask at the end of the interview, there are lots of suggestions available on the internet.

Afterword

I hope that you have found this self-help book useful and informative.

The main purpose of the book is to encourage you to create your own 'Interview Questions and Answers' document.

To start with, add the 20 commonly asked interview questions from Section 3 of this book and write answers for each of them.

Before each interview, memorize and rehearse the answers that you have prepared. It is like learning your lines for a show: the more you rehearse the better your performance will be.

After each interview add any questions that you struggled with into the 'Interview Questions and Answers' document, produce good answers and learn them.

Can you see, that by following this process you cannot fail but to get better and better with each interview?

It is a really simple concept but it works!

I wish you every success in your job hunt and remember: if you don't get the job don't be too disappointed - learn from the experience and prepare better answers ready for next time.

If you follow the process described in this book then someday soon I guarantee you are going to get that job!

Good Luck!

Review and Feedback

If you have found this book useful please be kind enough to leave a positive review.

In addition, I would love to receive any comments or feedback on this self-help book. Please send them to the following email address:

matthewjburgessbook@gmail.com

www.ingramcontent.com/pod-product-compliance
Lightning Source LLC
Chambersburg PA
CBHW071807170526
45167CB00003B/1203